A LIFEGUIDE® BIBLE STUDY

OLD TESTAMENT
K I N G S

12 Studies
for individuals or groups

Carolyn Nystrom

With Notes for Leaders

INTERVARSITY PRESS
DOWNERS GROVE, ILLINOIS 60515

InterVarsity Press® is the book-publishing division of InterVarsity Christian Fellowship®, a student movement active on campus at hundreds of universities, colleges and schools of nursing in the United States of America, and a member movement of the International Fellowship of Evangelical Students. For information about local and regional activities, write Public Relations Dept., InterVarsity Christian Fellowship, 6400 Schroeder Rd., P.O. Box 7895, Madison, WI 53707-7895.

LifeGuide® is a registered trademark of InterVarsity Christian Fellowship.

Cover photograph: Ted and Gwendolyn Brand

ISBN 0-8308-1070-6

Printed in the United States of America ♾

18	17	16	15	14	13	12	11	10	9	8	7	5	4	3	2	1
06	05	04	03	02	01	00	99	98	97	96	95	94	93			

Contents

Getting the Most
from LifeGuide® Bible Studies

Many of us long to fill our minds and our lives with Scripture. We desire to be transformed by its message. LifeGuide® Bible Studies are designed to be an exciting and challenging way to do just that. They help us to be guided by God's Word in every area of life.

How They Work
LifeGuides have a number of distinctive features. Perhaps the most important is that they are *inductive* rather than *deductive*. In other words, they lead us to *discover* what the Bible says rather than simply *telling* us what it says.

They are also thought-provoking. They help us to think about the meaning of the passage so that we can truly understand what the author is saying. The questions require more than one-word answers.

The studies are personal. Questions expose us to the promises, assurances, exhortations and challenges of God's Word. They are designed to allow the Scriptures to renew our minds so that we can be transformed by the Spirit of God. This is the ultimate goal of all Bible study.

The studies are versatile. They are designed for student, neighborhood and church groups. They are also effective for individual study.

How They're Put Together
LifeGuides also have a distinctive format. Each study need take no more than forty-five minutes in a group setting or thirty minutes in personal study—unless you choose to take more time.

The studies can be used within a quarter system in a church and fit well in a semester or trimester system on a college campus. If a guide has more than thirteen studies, it is divided into two or occasionally three parts of approximately twelve studies each.

LifeGuides use a workbook format. Space is provided for writing answers to each question. This is ideal for personal study and allows group members to prepare in advance for the discussion. The studies also contain leader's notes. They show how to lead a group discussion, provide additional background information on certain questions, give helpful tips on group dynamics and suggest ways to deal with problems which may arise during the discussion. With such helps, someone with little or no experience can lead an effective study.

Suggestions for Individual Study

1. As you begin each study, pray that God will help you to understand and apply the passage to your life.

2. Read and reread the assigned Bible passage to familiarize yourself with what the author is saying. In the case of book studies, you may want to read through the entire book prior to the first study. This will give you a helpful overview of its contents.

3. A good modern translation of the Bible, rather than the King James Version or a paraphrase, will give you the most help. The New International Version, the New American Standard Bible and the Revised Standard Version are all recommended. However, the questions in this guide are based on the New International Version.

4. Write your answers in the space provided in the study guide. This will help you to express your understanding of the passage clearly.

5. It might be good to have a Bible dictionary handy. Use it to look up any unfamiliar words, names or places.

Suggestions for Group Study

1. Come to the study prepared. Follow the suggestions for individual study mentioned above. You will find that careful preparation will greatly enrich your time spent in group discussion.

2. Be willing to participate in the discussion. The leader of your group will not be lecturing. Instead, he or she will be encouraging the members of the group to discuss what they have learned from the passage. The leader will be asking the questions that are found in this guide. Plan to share what God has taught you in your individual study.

3. Stick to the passage being studied. Your answers should be based on the verses which are the focus of the discussion and not on outside authorities such as commentaries or speakers. This guide deliberately avoids jumping from book to book or passage to passage. Each study focuses on only one

passage. Book studies are generally designed to lead you through the book in the order in which it was written. This will help you follow the author's argument.

4. Be sensitive to the other members of the group. Listen attentively when they share what they have learned. You may be surprised by their insights! Link what you say to the comments of others so the group stays on the topic. Also, be affirming whenever you can. This will encourage some of the more hesitant members of the group to participate.

5. Be careful not to dominate the discussion. We are sometimes so eager to share what we have learned that we leave too little opportunity for others to respond. By all means participate! But allow others to also.

6. Expect God to teach you through the passage being discussed and through the other members of the group. Pray that you will have an enjoyable and profitable time together.

7. If you are the discussion leader, you will find additional suggestions and helpful ideas for each study in the leader's notes. These are found at the back of the guide.

Introducing Old Testament Kings

What good will it do us twentieth-century Christians to study the kings who ruled a nation of Hebrews three thousand years ago? For people who get excited about battles and dates and ancient political maneuverings, the answer is obvious. All history, even Hebrew history, is great.

But what about the rest of us? God must have had some reason for designing his Holy Book so that one-third of the Old Testament text recounts historical events. He wasn't just entertaining history buffs. A look at the issues surrounding these kings will give us some clues.

We see Solomon, who prayed as if he knew exactly what God desired to give, then fell into paganism under the influence of his 700 (!) wives. And we ask, "Do I ever place the people I love ahead of God?"

We see Jeroboam and Rehoboam, who split their nation in civil war and then split their places of worship. (Who among us has endured civil war within our church that could end in separate places of worship?)

We see Asa, who looked for God with all of his might, and Ahab, who ignored God even though prophets shouted into his spiritually deaf ears. And we ask, "Who among us has looked for God and delighted in the finding?" Even so, we look with dread on our own potential deafness.

We see Jehoshaphat, who cried out to God that he couldn't fight another inch. And we watch God fight the battle for him. So we heave a sigh at our own weariness and ask the same God for battle help.

We see Ahaz, who, when faced with trouble, stopped believing in God. And we wonder about our own ability to keep faith in the face of circumstantial despair.

We see Hoshea, who angered God so much by his determination to serve other gods, that God terminated his nation. And we pray for our own national leaders, and thereby for ourselves. We see Hezekiah, who when faced with terminal illness, cried out to God. And God extended his life, which Hezekiah may have later regretted. And we wonder whether we will die with grace, or fear, or both.

We see Manasseh, the most wicked king of all. Yet God let him reign for forty-five years, the longest reign of any Hebrew king. We wonder how our faith, rattled by an afternoon of inconvenience, would endure an era when the king killed God-worshipers every day.

We see Josiah, who became a king at the age of eight, yet turned his nation to worship God. And we wonder about our influence for God on our own children—and the results of their influence on others.

We see Zedekiah, the last Hebrew king, presiding over a nation already dead. And we look for hope from a God who is not stopped by death.

They ruled for four centuries, these Hebrew kings. There were forty-two of them. Some ruled only days, others for a lifetime. Some were so minor that they rate only a line of text. Others fill whole books. Some were evil; some were good. The biblical text evaluates each one at the end of his life. A reminder that we, ourselves, will undergo the same evaluation.

But when the narrative of the kings ends with the fall of Judah in 587 B.C., their names are not forgotten. In the opening pages of the New Testament, they live again. It seems that when God chose a family for his Son, the infant Jesus, he chose from a line of kings. And so we read Joseph's genealogy, and we find, among all those hard-to-pronounce names, a familiar line: the Kings of Israel.

Let us read from them and learn. None was perfect, and neither are we. But God was sovereign—even over the kings. And he is sovereign over us as well.

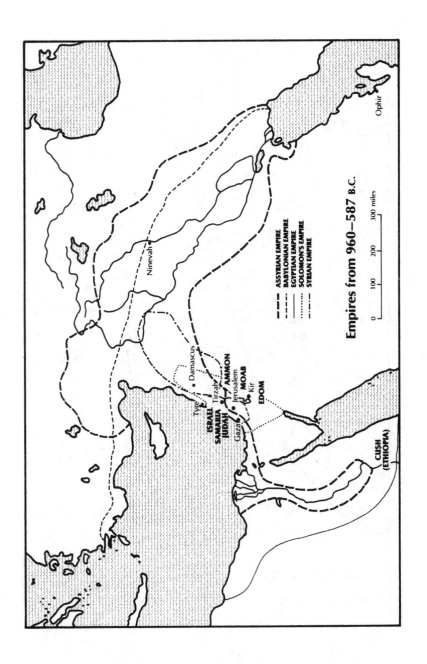

Ophir

Ninevah

ASSYRIAN EMPIRE
BABYLONIAN EMPIRE
EGYPTIAN EMPIRE
SOLOMON'S EMPIRE
SYRIAN EMPIRE

0   100   200   300 miles

Empires from 960–587 B.C.

Damascus

Tyre
Tirzah
Jerusalem
ISRAEL
SAMARIA
JUDAH
Gaza
AMMON
MOAB
Kir
EDOM

CUSH
(ETHIOPIA)

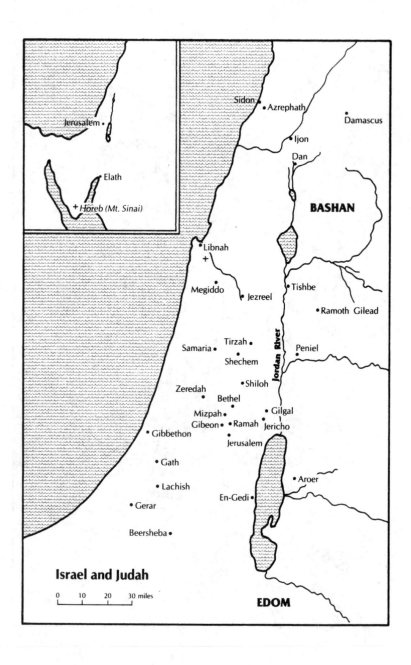

Sidon •
• Azrephath
Damascus
• Ijon
Dan •
BASHAN
Jerusalem •
Elath
+ Horeb (Mt. Sinai)
• Libnah
+
Megiddo •
• Jezreel
• Tishbe
• Ramoth Gilead
Jordan River
• Tirzah
Samaria •
Shechem •
Peniel
• Shiloh
Zeredah
•
• Bethel
Mizpah •
• Gilgal
Gibeon •
• Ramah
Jericho
Jerusalem •
• Gibbethon
• Aroer
• Gath
• Lachish
En-Gedi •
• Gerar
Beersheba •

Israel and Judah

0   10   20   30 miles

EDOM

1
Solomon: Praying with God's Values

1 Kings 3

Hello, Mary? I need a listening ear. Do you have time?"

Haltingly, I poured out my disappointment and sorrow about a problem that had been plaguing me for days. Mary made sympathetic noises, offered a few corrective comments, and promised to pray. The situation was unchanged; yet, as the day progressed, I felt the cloud of sadness lift. I knew Mary was praying. And God, in his generosity, was granting the requests of her prayer.

Why had I chosen Mary? Because she was approachable? Partly. But more because I knew her spiritual walk. It was carefully metered by God's laws. And because she was comfortable with prayer, her prayers were specific and to the point. Like her spiritual walk, her prayers seemed closely matched to God's values.

---

1. If you wanted someone to pray for you, who would you call?

Why would you choose that person?

2. Read 1 Kings 3:1-15. What were some of Solomon's actions in the early years of his reign (vv. 1-4)?

What do these actions say about Solomon's character?

---

3. Solomon answered God's question with a prayer (vv. 5-9). What does Solomon's prayer suggest about his attitude toward himself, his job and his God?

---

4. What did God promise Solomon (vv. 10-14)?

---

5. What conditions did God attach to granting Solomon a long life?

---

6. What changes did these promises bring in Solomon's behavior?

---

7. How would you describe a discerning heart?

8. Think of one of your current responsibilities that seems a bit too big for you just now. What would you *like* to ask of God in that area?

What *should* you ask of God?

9. Read 1 Kings 3:16-28. Imagine yourself as a bystander in King Solomon's court. What emotions would you feel during the different stages of the hearing?

10. Do you agree that Solomon's method of judgment was wise? Why, or why not?

11. In what specific ways does this show that God was answering Solomon's prayer (vv. 7-9)?

12. How can you begin to bring your prayers more into line with God's values?

13. Think of one person who particularly needs a discerning heart right now. Pray one or two sentences asking God's help for that person.

2
Solomon: Faithless in Love
1 Kings 11

I want to do God's will—if only I knew what it was," the young woman said to her pastor. "God has brought Bill and me together, and he has created a great love between us. Bill wants to marry me, but I'm not sure."

"But has Bill given himself to Jesus Christ?" her pastor probed.

"No, not yet," she hesitated. "But I think he will—perhaps after we're married . . ." Her voice trailed off under her pastor's firm gaze.

"God has already shown you his will, I think," her pastor replied. "You know Paul's writings to the Christians at Corinth: 'Do not be yoked together with unbelievers.' "

The young woman nodded reluctantly.

God's laws may seem harsh, but they are less harsh than the results of living by our own guidelines. God seems to know what works. Solomon had occasion to discover this truth.

---

1. What have you seen happen when spiritual values are kept separate from everyday life?

---

2. Read 1 Kings 11:1-25. What negative effects did wealth and power have on Solomon?

3. Why had God commanded his people not to intermarry with the nations around them (v. 2)?

4. In what ways did Solomon break the first commandment, "You shall have no other gods before me" (vv. 1-13)?

5. In verse 13 God says that the consequence of Solomon's sin will be that his kingdom will be taken away. What mercy does God promise? Why?

6. Solomon allowed his acquisition of wives to ease out his faith in God. When has your own love for a person created tensions with your faith?

7. How can we balance our love for the important people in our lives with our love for God?

8. What indications do you see that Hadad had the potential to become a serious threat to Solomon (vv. 14-22)?

What about Rezon (vv. 23-25)?

9. Read 1 Kings 11:26-43. How did God use Ahijah's new cloak as a message to Jeroboam (vv. 29-31)?

10. If Jeroboam chose to benefit from the experience of Israel's previous two kings, how would it affect his reign?

11. Verse 6 characterizes Solomon's life with the words, "So Solomon did evil in the eyes of the LORD." Why do you think God described such a successful king in this way?

12. If you were to name one sin that brought this description on Solomon, what would it be? Explain.

13. Solomon's marriages to pagans testified to his lack of wholehearted commitment to God. In what area of your life do you struggle to keep your actions in line with your beliefs?

3
Jeroboam/Rehoboam: Internal Conflict

1 Kings 12

Civil war. American minds turn to Yankee blue battling Confederate gray; brothers, cousins and neighbors pitted against each other; a wantonly destructive march to the sea—forever an embarrassment to both sides; a president on his knees, in tears.

Three thousand years ago, Israel, too, suffered civil war with many of the same griefs. As in the U.S. Civil War, family members had to decide which side they were on. Geography wasn't always the most important factor, for this war was not only a war of politics. It was also, at least at the outset, a war of faith.

1. How do you respond to conflict within your church or fellowship group?

How does that kind of conflict affect your faith?

2. Read 1 Kings 12:1-24. What steps in these verses led to the division recorded in verse 20?

3. At what points did reconciliation seem possible?

4. What volatile words and actions on both sides fanned the disagreement into open war (vv. 10-16)?

5. What indications do you find that God had not abandoned his people during this time of conflict?

6. If you had to go through a civil war, of what value would it be for you to know that nothing is outside the power of God?

7. Read 1 Kings 12:25-33. Looking at the map on page 14, what geographic reasons can you see for Jeroboam's selection of these sites?

8. What motivated Jeroboam to set up alternate places of worship (vv. 26-27)?

9. What spiritual results for the people of Israel would you expect to grow out of Jeroboam's new places of worship?

10. What did Jeroboam do that was contrary to God's law for his people? (Find all that you can in verses 31-33.)

11. If you were a godly person living under Jeroboam's rule, what choices would you have to make?

12. In what ways do your actions show a take-it-for-granted attitude toward your current opportunities to worship?

13. What steps could you take to worship God more fully?

4
Asa: Seeker of God
2 Chronicles 14—15

My friend "Susan," emotionally raw from a recent divorce, attended a Fourth of July picnic with some friends, only to discover that the one thing more lonely than being alone is being alone in a crowd. She came home feeling not only husbandless, but also that her life was without God. For twenty years she had willed God out of existence. Now, more alone than ever, she stretched out on her empty bed and spoke the hesitant beginnings of prayer, "God, if you are there . . ."

So began a tortuous journey toward faith—a seeking after God. And God heard her prayer; bit by bit, God Almighty revealed himself to Susan.

---

1. How have you seen people being drawn to God?

---

2. Read 2 Chronicles 14. List the action words in verses 1-7.

What do these words tell you about Asa?

3. What does Asa's prayer (v. 11) reveal about his relationship with God?

4. According to Asa's actions and his prayer, what are some things that he believed about God?

5. What events recorded in this chapter suggest that Asa's beliefs were correct?

6. How has God helped you to keep on believing in him?

7. Read 2 Chronicles 15. Looking at verses 1-7, what past conditions in Israel might cause Asa to listen carefully to God's message?

8. What warnings are implied in Azariah's prophecy?

what blessings?

9. What information can you gather from this prophecy about what God expects from his followers?

10. What words and phrases in 15:8-19 show the wholeheartedness with which Asa and his people turned to God?

11. What changes can you imagine in the day-to-day living of ordinary people because of this reform?

12. These chapters show that if you seek the Lord, he will be found by you. What does this suggest about the nature of spiritual development?

13. At your current stage of spiritual development, what steps could you take right now to seek the Lord?

5
Ahab: Deaf to God
1 Kings 22:1-40

A commuter spinning the dial of a car radio catches a few words from a British preacher and quickly moves on.

We each have our own methods of tuning out God. For example, singing an entire hymn without a single word registering in the mind; meticulously compiling a things-to-do list during the sermon; accidentally leaving a Bible at church and not missing it for days; feeling no compunction about a pattern of daily prayer long since abandoned and hardly remembered.

There are many paths by which we can become deaf to God. Ahab's life (and death) warns us against such a route.

1. What do you do that sometimes makes you "deaf" to God?

2. Read 1 Kings 21:17-19. Why do you think that God gave Ahab this information?

3. Read 1 Kings 22:1-28. List all the characters in this drama.

Why is each one important to the story?

4. What was Ahab the king of Israel's proposal (vv. 1-4)?

5. How did the two kings view the project differently?

6. What was hard about Micaiah's job?

7. Look again at Micaiah's statements in verses 17-23. Why do you think that Ahab was an easy prey for the lying prophets?

8. What did it cost Micaiah to speak God's truth?

9. Why do you sometimes hesitate to talk about what you know to be God's truth?

10. What responsibilities seem to accompany familiarity with God?

---

11. Read 1 Kings 22:29-40. Ahab had many opportunities for hearing truths from God in the course of his life. In view of this, what do you see as the difference between hearing and receiving God's Word?

---

12. What precautions could you take to keep from acquiring Ahab's kind of deafness?

6
Jehoshaphat: Battle Weary

2 Chronicles 20:1-30

Battles in Jehoshaphat's life took the form of armies marching across the Palestinian wilderness, bloody conflicts in the valleys, hunting and hiding in the mountains. My battles are of a different kind. They are often battles of time: four children, countless ensemble rehearsals for the girls, sports practices for the boys, two weekly Bible studies, a prayer group, a seventy-family Sunday school to superintend, a weepy neighbor to console, music practice to oversee ("No, a dotted half gets three beats"), homework to enforce, a neglected manuscript scattered over the dining-room table. I am battle weary.

I once experienced God's momentary deliverance from this battle. It took the form of a Midwestern snowstorm. Each jingle of the phone announced a cancellation. Our family had a day to relax, lounging around a popping fire with the chords of Handel's *Messiah* in the background. I did not have to fight the battle that day.

1. When do you feel weary?

2. Read 2 Chronicles 20:1-30. How did Jehoshaphat and his people respond to the news of the army's approach?

3. What elements of praise do you find in Jehoshaphat's prayer (vv. 6-12)?

4. What reasons did Jehoshaphat give God for dealing with this problem (vv. 7-10)?

Why did Jehoshaphat ask for God's judgment?

5. Imagine yourself standing in the crowd of people described in verse 13. How would you have felt about Jahaziel's words in verses 15-17? Why?

6. What risks would a person who truly believed this prophecy take?

7. In what different ways did the people of Judah worship God (vv. 18-30)?

8. What methods did God use to fulfill his prophecy of the previous day?

9. Why do you think God answered Jehoshaphat's prayer in this way?

10. Notice the fear of God in surrounding kingdoms (v. 29). In what sense were they correct to say, "The LORD had fought against the enemies of Israel"?

_____

11. Look again at the words in 2 Chronicles 20:15-17: "For the battle is not yours. . . . You will not have to fight this battle." When do you most need to hear this kind of message from God?

_____

12. What can you learn from Jehoshaphat about the way to pray during such situations?

_____

13. God will not fight all of our battles for us. (He didn't fight all of Jehoshaphat's. Besides, we might even be in the wrong battle!) But what can you learn from Jehoshaphat's walk with God that will help you cope when you feel battle weary?

7
Ahaz: Faithless in Trouble

2 Kings 16

We had two girls, but we had planned two more children—boys, we hoped. Already, I had lost one baby in the first trimester. Pregnant again, I prayed my way through those first three months. Shortly into the second trimester the pregnancy was in trouble. I lost the baby.

And I was mad! I had done all the right things. I had been especially careful about diet, medicines, activities. I had prayed constantly. But the baby had died inside me anyway. I prayed one angry prayer to God and then stopped praying altogether. For a while.

But God is merciful. He gave us two boys (adopted). Later I had to ask, "Why was I so mad? Is God only God for the good times? Is he a handy tool for me to get what I want and to lay aside when he (in my view) doesn't deliver?" My response to trouble was not so different from that of King Ahaz. When the going got tough, Ahaz switched sides.

---

1. When is it hard for you to have faith in God?

---

2. Read 2 Kings 16:1-20. In what different ways did Ahaz express his idolatry?

3. What military crisis did Ahaz face (vv. 5-6)? (Use your map to picture this.)

4. Why do you think Ahaz appealed to Assyria?

5. What did help from Assyria cost the people of Judah?

6. What reasons did Ahaz have to be wary of this alliance?

7. What specific changes did Ahaz make in the temple?

8. God gave Moses specific instructions for arrangements in his tabernacle. In view of this, what was Ahaz saying by his actions in the temple?

9. Think of difficult times you have experienced, for example, a fight within your church, the death of someone you have prayed for, unemployment, family or friends going through a divorce. What are some negative ways you have responded to such situations?

What are some positive ways you have responded?

---

10. In what ways does your response to trouble seem to be a search for other gods and other altars?

To what extent does your response to trouble reflect a determined faith in God?

---

11. Much of our worship can become, like Ahaz's, an attempt to get what we want out of God. When this occurs, we need to ask ourselves, "Who is my god: God or me?" How can you make your worship less self-centered and more God-centered?

8
Hoshea: Idolatry's Reward

2 Kings 17

We had just bought a new house, a three-bedroom ranch on an acre of land. I could plant fruit trees and a vegetable garden. Our children could run and yell without disturbing neighbors. Our kitchen was big enough for two people to work together, and all six of us could sit down at the table. Best of all, there were windows everywhere.

When my brother visited, he asked matter-of-factly, "Is this house your goal in life?" He meant, "Do you plan to stay here, or are you planning to 'move up'?"

I knew what he meant, but I chose to answer what he actually asked. "No, of course not," I said stoutly. "I don't think any house could be my goal in life."

I could answer with confidence because I'm just not a house person, as my grubby kitchen floor and cluttered linen closet will testify. But had Dan chosen another topic (such as work, friends, family, church), I might have had to squirm a little. Idolatry is insidious to us all.

---

1. How would you define idolatry?

---

2. Read 2 Kings 17. How does this chapter make you feel?

3. Notice the people and places in verses 1-6. How do these verses outline the final steps to Israel's death as a nation?

4. Why was the Assyrian technique of conquering an effective way to wipe out a nation (vv. 1-6, 24)?

5. Review the list of sins (there are about twenty) in verses 7-22. What common characteristics do you find?

6. How would you summarize Israel's sin in one sentence?

7. The writer of 2 Kings says repeatedly of Israel, "The LORD removed them from his presence." Consider the events of this chapter. What did it mean to Israel in practical terms to be removed from the presence of God (vv. 18, 20 and 23)?

8. Do you think that it is possible for people or nations today to be removed from the presence of God? Explain.

9. Notice the references to Judah, Israel's sister nation to the south. If you had been living in Judah at the time of the events recorded here, what might you have learned about the relationship of God to his chosen people?

_____

10. Why did Israel find it hard to serve one God alone (vv. 14-17)?

Why did the new Samaritans find it so hard (vv. 24-33)?

_____

11. We too are vulnerable to serving "other gods." Take a private inventory of your own temptations by jotting down answers to the following questions:
I couldn't live without _____.
When my mind is idle, it automatically turns to _____.
If I could have anything in the world, I would choose _____.
The most important thing (or person) to me is _____.
I know God wants me to _____, but I can't.
In view of your inventory, in what areas of your life do you need to be alert to the temptation of idolatry?

_____

12. What steps can you take to keep normal healthy interests in the world around you from turning into idolatry?

9
Hezekiah: King in Crisis
Isaiah 36—37

Taunts. With two sons less than a year apart, I've heard my share of them. Two boys crouch over small toy cars that zoom down newly created roads in the dirt. But this peaceful scene is too often interrupted by, "Hey! Quit muckin' up my road!"

"It's not your road. I made it."

"Well, my car's on it, so it's my road."

"Hey, that's not your car; it's mine. See—mine had the wobbly front wheel."

"My wheel got wobbly too. Hey, get your knee out of the road. You're wreckin' it. Da-ad!"

"Dad's not gonna do anything. I'll tell him you took my car. Da-ad!"

Small issues. Small children, each convinced that Dad will take his side. But when nations play such taunting games, thousands of lives are at stake. And if one king is correct when he says to another, "Your God's not going to help you; he's on my side," a whole nation may go into crisis. It may disappear as quickly as a finger-width dirt road beneath a careless knee.

---

1. What is one of your typical ways of dealing with crisis?

---

2. Read Isaiah 36. Notice the people and places in verses 1-4. How do they help you define what was about to happen?

3. What reasons did Hezekiah have to take this meeting seriously? (See verses 4-10, as well as 2 Kings 18:13-16.)

4. In what ways did the Assyrian field commander misuse truth to undermine Hezekiah's people (vv. 11-22)?

5. If you had been on the wall listening to this conversation, what would you have worried about?

6. Three times the Assyrian commander taunted his Hebrew listeners with the threat that their Lord would not protect them from his attacks. When have you worried about God's apparent lack of protection?

7. Read Isaiah 37:1-20. What words and phrases show that Hezekiah took the Assyrian threat seriously (vv. 1-8)?

8. Notice the dialogue and activities throughout verses 1-20. In what sense was this a spiritual as well as a political confrontation?

Would the spiritual dimension bring comfort or fear to Hezekiah? Why?

9. How was Hezekiah's response to the Assyrian letter rooted in the character of God? (Notice both words and actions.)

---

10. Read Isaiah 37:21-38. How might Isaiah's song help you to worship God during a time of crisis?

---

11. This message from Isaiah is often called a "taunt song." In what ways did it rebut the Assyrian taunts that Hezekiah had endured?

---

12. What do the final events in verses 36-38 contribute to this story's revelations about God?

---

13. In what ways is Hezekiah a good model for handling crises?

---

14. Take a moment now to write a brief statement of your own most recent personal crisis. Spread it, in prayer, before God.

10
Manasseh: One Giant Step Backward
2 Kings 20:1—21:18

My friends Bob and Dottie and their children are missionaries to a primitive tribe of Indians in South America. After some initial awkwardness, they were well received. They donned the long white tunics of the tribal people, carried their woven handbags, and wore tiny beaded necklaces. They washed clothing native-style by beating it on the riverside rocks. They carried their babies like papooses. (It was easier for climbing mountains.) They ate native food. The Indians helped Bob and Dottie learn the language. They came for medical help when they were sick or wounded. God seemed ready to use them to help bring these people into his kingdom.

Then drug traffic swept the area. Speculators bought the land or simply massacred Indians reluctant to sell. Twentieth-century viruses decimated the tribe. Bob and his young son were falsely arrested and jailed. The area had become too dangerous for mission work. In fact, only two-thirds of the Indians remained alive. And some who were left looked at them with hostile eyes.

Can we still trust God when all the trends point counter to what we know of his purposes? One of the advantages of studying the Old Testament is seeing, in a few pages, God moving through hundreds of years of history. It may help us trust God's unseen purposes for our own small page.

---

1. What popular cultural trends seem to go against God's standard of what is right?

2. Read 2 Kings 20:1-21. What do the details in the communication between God and Hezekiah reveal about their relationship (vv. 1-11)?

3. Why do you think Hezekiah treated the messengers from Babylon the way he did (vv. 12-21)?

4. What connections did Isaiah find between Hezekiah's actions and the future of Judah?

5. In view of your picture of Hezekiah's prayer in the previous study, how would you expect him to respond to this prophecy from Isaiah?

What explanation can you offer for the response recorded here?

6. Read 2 Kings 21:1-18. When you try to imagine life in Judah under Manasseh's reign, what pictures come to your mind?

7. Find as many references to the people of Judah as you can in 21:7-15. How do these help explain why Manasseh was able to make such a total reversal of his father's reforms?

8. What does the prophet's use of symbols help illustrate about the future?

9. Suppose you were living in Judah at this time. You heard this prophecy and believed it to be true. What would you do?

10. Why do you think no Old Testament prophet claims to have written during Manasseh's reign?

11. Look back at Hezekiah's situation in 2 Kings 20:1-11. If Hezekiah could have known the future, including the birth of his son, do you think he would have wanted God to add fifteen years to his life? Why, or why not?

12. What do you know about God that helps you to stand against popular trends that go against what you know is right?

13. How can you serve God in your response to these trends?

11
Josiah: Following God's Law

2 Kings 22:1—23:30

Seniors in high school typically get a little huffy about restrictive school rules such as hall passes and washroom permits. Sometimes even teachers are not immune to similar feelings.

When my daughter's music teacher, accustomed to working with diligent honors students, was confronted with the request for one more hall pass for an in-building errand, he wrote, "Sheri has my permission to be in the hall so that she can check the drug supply in her locker. Antonia is her bodyguard." (They weren't stopped.)

There's something inside us that grates against laws—of any kind—unless, of course, we've had to live a long time without them. Judah had such an experience.

---

1. What rules annoyed you during your own teen years?

Why do you think so many of us bristle at rules and laws?

2. Read 2 Kings 22:1—23:3. What steps led to finding the Book of the Law (22:1-8)?

3. What can you know about Huldah from verses 14-20?

What could Josiah know about God from her message?

4. What effect would you expect the scene in 23:1-3 to have on the people?

5. Read 2 Kings 23:4-30. These verses list some sixteen religious reforms that Josiah instituted. As you read through these reforms, what do you learn about the spiritual practices of the people before Josiah became king?

6. How would you expect the life of an ordinary person to be affected by these changes?

7. Much of today's culture ignores God's laws. What pressures do you feel to follow the culture rather than the law of God?

8. In what different ways did Josiah show respect for the law of God? (Draw from all of 2 Kings 22—23.)

9. What words and phrases describe Josiah in verse 25?

10. What relationship do you see between our response to God's law and our concept of God?

11. Study more carefully the words in 2 Kings 23:25 describing Josiah's commitment to God and to God's law. What aspect of that description would you like to make more a part of your own commitment?

12. God's law is tied to his character. As you think of your own natural resistance to law, what steps could you take to bring your response to God's law into line with what you believe to be true of God?

12
Zedekiah: End of the Line

2 Kings 24:1—25:21

Ezekiel 8
Dig you prophet, Dig in the wall
Probe the hole that opens to the night
Weep Ezekiel, Weep for your call

Crumble small the whitewash with your awl
Daubed by holy priests who smothered light
Dig you prophet, Dig in the wall

Dig you deeper, Dig back to the fall
Hasten shepherd, see your flock's in flight
Weep Ezekiel, Weep for your call

Hide your eyes and shrink from the small
Door that dries your bones as if you might
Not dig. You watchman, Dig in the wall

Seventy elders, sentries of God's law
Worship beasts and creatures slimed with blight
Weep Ezekiel, Weep for your call

Watch the Spirit flee among the tall
Cherubim, who bear Him out of sight
Hear the curse of God upon your wall
Weep you watchman, Weep for your call
                              —*Carolyn Nystrom, 1980*

1. How do you feel when a Christian leader falls deep into sin?

_____

2. Read 2 Kings 24:1—25:21. How does this account of the fall of God's nation make you feel? Why?

_____

3. Using the material you've read, trace the final steps of the nation of Judah.

_____

4. What events in those final years make the strongest impression on your mind?

Why do these events seem especially haunting?

_____

5. Look more carefully at 2 Kings 24:3-4 and 20. What cautions might these words bring to your own life?

_____

6. Consider the history of Israel and Judah. What turning points do you see that led to this kind of end?

7. How might this study of Jewish history affect the way you pray for your own nation and its leaders?

_____

8. For what specific national needs or leaders should you be praying?

_____

9. Take time now to pray together for the needs and people you have just discussed.

_____

10. During the time that Zedekiah and his people were about to be deported to Babylon, the prophet Jeremiah wrote a letter to the Hebrew people already captive in Babylon. Read God's words to them in Jeremiah 29:10-14. If you had been a Hebrew captive in Babylon, what effect would these words have on the way you conducted your life during captivity?

_____

11. What does this passage reveal about the character of God?

_____

12. What personal hope do these words from Jeremiah offer to you?

Leader's Notes

Leading a Bible discussion can be an enjoyable and rewarding experience. But it can also be *scary*—especially if you've never done it before. If this is your feeling, you're in good company. When God asked Moses to lead the Israelites out of Egypt, he replied, "O Lord, please send someone else to do it!" (Ex 4:13).

When Solomon became king of Israel, he felt the task was beyond his abilities. "I am only a little child and do not know how to carry out my duties. . . . Who is able to govern this great people of yours?" (1 Kings 3:7, 9).

When God called Jeremiah to be a prophet, he replied, "Ah, Sovereign LORD, . . . I do not know how to speak; I am only a child" (Jer 1:6).

The list goes on. The apostles were "unschooled, ordinary men" (Acts 4:13). Timothy was young, frail and frightened. Paul's "thorn in the flesh" made him feel weak. But God's response to all of his servants—including you—is essentially the same: "My grace is sufficient for you" (2 Cor 12:9). Relax. God helped these people in spite of their weaknesses, and he can help you in spite of your feelings of inadequacy.

There is another reason why you should feel encouraged. Leading a Bible discussion is not difficult if you follow certain guidelines. You don't need to be an expert on the Bible or a trained teacher. The suggestions listed below should enable you to effectively and enjoyably fulfill your role as leader.

Preparing to Lead

1. Ask God to help you understand and apply the passage to your own life. Unless this happens, you will not be prepared to lead others. Pray too for the various members of the group. Ask God to give you an enjoyable and profitable time together studying his Word.

2. As you begin each study, read and reread the assigned Bible passage to familiarize yourself with what the author is saying. In the case of book studies, you may want to read through the entire book prior to the first study. This will give you a helpful overview of its contents.

3. This study guide is based on the New International Version of the Bible. It will help you and the group if you use this translation as the basis for your study and discussion. Encourage others to use the NIV also, but allow them the freedom to use whatever translation they prefer.

4. Carefully work through each question in the study. Spend time in meditation and reflection as you formulate your answers.

5. Write your answers in the space provided in the study guide. This will help you to express your understanding of the passage clearly.

6. It might help you to have a Bible dictionary handy. Use it to look up any unfamiliar words, names or places. (For additional help on how to study a passage, see chapter five of *Leading Bible Discussions,* IVP.)

7. Once you have finished your own study of the passage, familiarize yourself with the leader's notes for the study you are leading. These are designed to help you in several ways. First, they tell you the purpose the study guide author had in mind while writing the study. Take time to think through how the study questions work together to accomplish that purpose. Second, the notes provide you with additional background information or comments on some of the questions. This information can be useful if people have difficulty understanding or answering a question. Third, the leader's notes can alert you to potential problems you may encounter during the study.

8. If you wish to remind yourself of anything mentioned in the leader's notes, make a note to yourself below that question in the study.

Leading the Study

1. Begin the study on time. Unless you are leading an evangelistic Bible study, open with prayer, asking God to help you to understand and apply the passage.

2. Be sure that everyone in your group has a study guide. Encourage them to prepare beforehand for each discussion by working through the questions in the guide.

3. At the beginning of your first time together, explain that these studies are meant to be discussions not lectures. Encourage the members of the group to participate. However, do not put pressure on those who may be hesitant to speak during the first few sessions.

4. Read the introductory paragraph at the beginning of the discussion. This will orient the group to the passage being studied.

5. Read the passage aloud if you are studying one chapter or less. You may choose to do this yourself, or someone else may read if he or she has been asked to do so prior to the study. Longer passages may occasionally be read in parts at different times during the study. Some studies may cover several chapters. In such cases reading aloud would probably take too much time, so the group members should simply read the assigned passages prior to the study.

6. As you begin to ask the questions in the guide, keep several things in mind. First, the questions are designed to be used just as they are written. If you wish, you may simply read them aloud to the group. Or you may prefer to express them in your own words. However, unnecessary rewording of the questions is not recommended.

Second, the questions are intended to guide the group toward understanding and applying the *main idea* of the passage. The author of the guide has stated his or her view of this central idea in the *purpose* of the study in the leader's notes. You should try to understand how the passage expresses this idea and how the study questions work together to lead the group in that direction.

There may be times when it is appropriate to deviate from the study guide. For example, a question may have already been answered. If so, move on to the next question. Or someone may raise an important question not covered in the guide. Take time to discuss it! The important thing is to use discretion. There may be many routes you can travel to reach the goal of the study. But the easiest route is usually the one the author has suggested.

7. Avoid answering your own questions. If necessary, repeat or rephrase them until they are clearly understood. An eager group quickly becomes passive and silent if they think the leader will do most of the talking.

8. Don't be afraid of silence. People may need time to think about the question before formulating their answers.

9. Don't be content with just one answer. Ask, "What do the rest of you think?" or "Anything else?" until several people have given answers to the question.

10. Acknowledge all contributions. Try to be affirming whenever possible. Never reject an answer. If it is clearly wrong, ask, "Which verse led you to that conclusion?" or again, "What do the rest of you think?"

11. Don't expect every answer to be addressed to you, even though this will probably happen at first. As group members become more at ease, they will begin to truly interact with each other. This is one sign of a healthy discussion.

12. Don't be afraid of controversy. It can be very stimulating. If you don't resolve an issue completely, don't be frustrated. Move on and keep it in mind for later. A subsequent study may solve the problem. **13.** Stick to the passage under consideration. It should be the source for answering the questions. Discourage the group from unnecessary cross-referencing. Likewise, stick to the subject and avoid going off on tangents. **14.** Periodically summarize what the *group* has said about the passage. This helps to draw together the various ideas mentioned and gives continuity to the study. But don't preach. **15.** Conclude your time together with conversational prayer. Be sure to ask God's help to apply those things which you learned in the study. **16.** End on time.

Many more suggestions and helps are found in *Leading Bible Discussions* (IVP). Reading and studying through that would be well worth your time.

Components of Small Groups

A healthy small group should do more than study the Bible. There are four components you should consider as you structure your time together.

Nurture. Being a part of a small group should be a nurturing and edifying experience. You should grow in your knowledge and love of God and each other. If we are to properly love God, we must know and keep his commandments (Jn 14:15). That is why Bible study should be a foundational part of your small group. But you can be nurtured by other things as well. You can memorize Scripture, read and discuss a book, or occasionally listen to a tape of a good speaker.

Community. Most people have a need for close friendships. Your small group can be an excellent place to cultivate such relationships. Allow time for informal interaction before and after the study. Have a time of sharing during the meeting. Do fun things together as a group, such as a potluck supper or a picnic. Have someone bring refreshments to the meeting. Be creative!

Worship. A portion of your time together can be spent in worship and prayer. Praise God together for who he is. Thank him for what he has done and is doing in your lives and in the world. Pray for each other's needs. Ask God to help you to apply what you have learned. Sing hymns together.

Mission. Many small groups decide to work together in some form of outreach. This can be a practical way of applying what you have learned. You can host a series of evangelistic discussions for your friends or neighbors. You can visit people at a home for the elderly. Help a widow with cleaning or repair jobs around her home. Such projects can have a transforming influence on your group.

For a detailed discussion of the nature and function of small groups, read *Small Group Leaders' Handbook* or *Good Things Come in Small Groups* (both from IVP).

Study 1. Solomon: Praying with God's Values. 1 Kings 3.
Purpose: To learn to pray within the context of God's values.
Question 1. Every study begins with an "approach" question, which is meant to be asked before the passage is read. These questions are important for several reasons.

First, they help the group to warm up to each other. No matter how well a group may know each other, there is always a stiffness that needs to be overcome before people will begin to talk openly. A good question will break the ice.

Second, approach questions get people thinking along the lines of the topic of the study. Most people will have lots of different things going on in their minds (dinner, an important meeting coming up, how to get the car fixed) that will have nothing to do with the study. A creative question will get their attention and draw them into the discussion.

Third, approach questions can reveal where our thoughts or feelings need to be transformed by Scripture. That is why it is especially important not to read the passage before the approach question is asked. The passage will tend to color the honest reactions people would otherwise give because they are, of course, supposed to think the way the Bible does. Giving honest responses before they find out what the Bible says may help them see where their thoughts or attitudes need to be changed.

Try to involve each person present with this question.
Question 2. If your group wishes to evaluate some of Solomon's early actions, refer them to Deuteronomy 12:1-7.
Question 3. Key words and phrases include: "servant" (vv. 7, 8, 9), "little child" (v. 7), "duties" (v. 7), "O Lord" (v. 7), "great people" (v. 8), "chosen" (v. 8), and "people of yours" (v. 9).
Question 10. Your group might speculate on the possible outcome if both women had protested the slaughter, if neither had, or if the wrong woman had protested.
Question 12. Encourage people to mention specific and concrete actions that would lead in that direction. Be sure to include prayers of worship and confession as well as prayers of petition. After Solomon asked (correctly) of God, he worshiped and made a sacrifice.

Question 13. Keep your prayers brief. Each person may pray more than once if he or she wants. Allow time for everyone to add something to these sentence prayers.

Study 2. Solomon: Faithless in Love. 1 Kings 11.
Purpose: To make our love for God even more important than our love for any person.

Question 7. Refer, if necessary, to Exodus 20:3. God gives us, as a precious gift, the beauty of human love. Even so, he demands that we give our highest allegiance to him alone. Help your group discuss ways to enjoy this human love (within its proper limits) but still keep God first.

Question 9. Notice that God had already given this message to Solomon (vv. 11-13). A question about the number of tribes may arise. Ten plus one did not equal twelve by the math in Solomon's time either! *The New Bible Commentary* suggests that the tribe of Judah eventually absorbed the nearby tribe of Simeon. Therefore, Solomon was to lose the northern ten tribes but retain the southern two tribes that eventually became one tribe—Judah.

Question 10. Notice the promises God makes in verses 35 and 37 and the conditions in verse 38.

Question 12. Idolatry, intermarriage, rebellion and self-centeredness are some of the sins that might have been root causes of Solomon's spiritual fall.

Question 13. Confession is always hard, so don't expect graphic details. Encourage several people to mention at least one general area in which God is convicting them.

Study 3. Jeroboam/Rehoboam: Internal Conflict. 1 Kings 12.
Purpose: To worship God in spite of conflict within our worship groups.

Question 2. Answers should be detailed and in sequence. Citing verse numbers will help the group to stay together. Someone should point out where the two leaders were at the beginning of the chapter and why.

Question 3. In defense of Rehoboam's harsh answer, the proper place for inauguration was Jerusalem. Yet Rehoboam went to Shechem in the North, probably because the people there would not come south to Jerusalem.

Notice Jeroboam's swift return from exile in Egypt—a hostile signal to Rehoboam. Notice also Adoniram, his position and his death.

Question 4. See verses 10-11, then 14-15 and finally 16.

Question 5. Verse 15 refers to 1 Kings 11:30-31. The events of verses 22-24 prevented unnecessary bloodshed.

Question 8. These two places of false worship (Bethel and Dan) appear again and again throughout the next two hundred years of Jewish history. They eventually become a partial cause for the separation of the Jews of Judah and a people later called the Samaritans.

Question 10. This question assumes some knowledge of the law as given in Exodus and Deuteronomy. Find several ways in which Jeroboam disobeyed God in these verses.

Question 12. Frequency of church attendance is only one area to discuss. Think also about the way you use opportunities for fellowship with other believers. (Do you fight over petty issues when you should be enjoying oneness in Christ?) And what do you actually do and think during worship—public as well as private?

Question 13. Use this question to encourage several group members to plan more effective use of their opportunities to worship.

Study 4. Asa: Seeker of God. 2 Chronicles 14—15.
Purpose: To know God better by continually seeking him.

Question 2. Ask each person to name one action word (verb) in these verses. Then discuss what these actions reveal about Asa's character.

Question 4. Your group should find a half-dozen or more implied beliefs. For example, Asa believed that God allows himself to be found by people—or he would not have commanded his people to "seek the Lord."

Question 5. Answers appear in verses 6, 7, 12 and 14.

Question 10. As you prepare to lead the discussion on this passage, circle in your Bible all the verbs and verb phrases in verses 8-19. This will help you see if your group is being thorough as it discusses this question.

Question 11. Encourage images of everyday life that would reflect this kind of massive reform. (Group members will probably include images of those who reformed willingly as well as those who were forced to reform.)

Canaanite religion presents us with no pretty picture. . . . Female deities included Asherah. . . . These Goddesses, though fluid in personality and function, represented the female principle in the fertility cult. They are portrayed as sacred courtesans or pregnant mothers or, with a surprising polarity, as blood thirsty goddesses of war. . . . As in all such religions, numerous debasing practices, including sacred prostitution, homosexuality and various orgiastic rites, were prevalent. It was the sort of religion with which Israel, however much she might borrow from the culture of Canaan, could never with good conscience make peace. (John Bright, *A History of Israel,* 3rd ed. [Philadelphia: Westminster Press, 1981], pp. 118-19)

Question 12. If people have trouble with this question, try smaller questions such as: "How is this phrase different from, 'If you seek him, you will find him'?" "What is your part?" "What is God's part?" "What does the process of seeking and finding involve?"

Question 13. Since spiritual development is a lifelong process, even those who have known God for a long time must still seek him in practical ways. Linger on this question long enough for several people to speak briefly of steps they might take if they wanted to become more diligent in seeking the Lord.

Study 5. Ahab: Deaf to God. 1 Kings 22:1-40.

Purpose: To act on what we know of God and thereby resist spiritual deafness.

Question 2. If your study time allows for it, you may want to begin by paging through the recorded events of Ahab's life in 1 Kings 16:29—21:29. Ask, "What opportunities did Ahab have to know God?" Opportunities can be found in 17:1, 7; 18:1, 17, 20-21, 30-38, 44-45; 20:42. Be sure that someone points out Elijah's confrontation and prophecy of 21:17-19.

Question 4. Your character list should include Ahab, Jehoshaphat, Zedekiah, a messenger, 400 prophets, Micaiah and the Lord.

Question 5. Find Ramoth Gilead on your map. Notice that it was on or near a major trade route.

Verse 2 reads, "Jehoshaphat . . . went down to see the king of Israel." Here, as throughout Kings and Chronicles, people travel down from Jerusalem— even if they are headed north. This is because Jerusalem is at high elevation. To travel anywhere is down.

Question 6. For background on the relationship between Israel and Aram (Syria), review quickly 1 Kings 20. Note particularly the terms of the treaty (v. 34) between Ahab and Ben-Hadad.

Question 8. If your group has trouble coming to the point, rephrase the question to ask, "What do these words reveal about God's purposes in these events?" They should notice that God was in control, even of the lying prophets. And that God had determined to send Ahab to his death by this means.

Question 9. See especially verses 13-14, 24 and 26-27.

Question 11. With this question begin to move the discussion into a twenti-eth-century framework.

Questions 12-13. Pace your study so that about ten minutes remain for these application questions.

Study 6. Jehoshaphat: Battle Weary. 2 Chronicles 20:1-30.

Purpose: To worship God because of his constant presence—even in circumstances that would otherwise overwhelm us.

Question 2. You should find a number of ways throughout the passage that Jehoshaphat, and then the people, responded to the problem.

Question 3. Praise occurs throughout the prayer, but several forms are found in verse 6.

Question 10. In verse 29 and elsewhere in Chronicles, the writer often refers to Judah as Israel. By this he is not confusing the two kingdoms, but insisting that only the section of the nation that follows God is worthy of the ancient name Israel.

Question 13. Be sure discussion at this point focuses on applications to the present—not to the ancient times of Jehoshaphat.

Study 7. Ahaz: Faithless in Trouble. 2 Kings 16.
Purpose: To trust God—even when he does not give us what we want.

Questions 3-4. Read Isaiah 7:1-12 for more information.

Question 6. Check the map for changes in the Assyrian borders. By forming an alliance with the most dangerous nation in the area, Ahaz had brought Assyrian borders to his own doorstep. Group members should also notice, in verse 9, the treatment a conquered nation could expect from Assyria. Ahaz had also been guilty, before God, of turning his sister nation (Israel) over to a common enemy. Participants may find other reasons that grow out of this passage.

Question 8. See Exodus 26:30 and 1 Chronicles 28:19 for more information.

Question 10. Group members should respond to these questions in a way that fits their own troublesome situations. Possible attempts to find "other gods and other altars" in the sample situations might include: I would leave my church that is in turmoil; I would stop praying for a while when my friend dies; I would express excessive anger at my spouse, assuming he or she, not God, is to take care of me; I would put *all* my faith in counseling as an aid to my friends who are getting divorced, not putting it in its proper perspective as one of the gifts from a living God who hates divorce.

Study 8. Hoshea: Idolatry's Reward. 2 Kings 17.
Purpose: To examine our lives for temptation toward idolatry.

Question 2. Invite everyone present to answer this question in some way. Ask several to explain why they feel the way they do.

Question 3. Someone may point out the apparent time discrepancy between 2 Kings 15:30 and 17:1. In their *Old Testament Commentaries,* Carl F. Keil and Franz Delitzsch explain this by suggesting that in this turbulent era an eight-year period of anarchy probably occurred before Hoshea was able to secure the throne (vol. 4, *First Kings—Esther*[Grand Rapids, Mich.: Eerdmans, 1971], p. 409).

Question 4. Notice the details of verses 1-6 as well as verse 24. Along with the other details, notice that Assyria imprisoned the Israeli king, captured the people of Israel, deported them to a land some six hundred miles away, and spread out the Jews so they could not form a cohesive group. To make sure there would be no vacant land to invite a return, Assyria, at the same time, imported other peoples to Samaria and settled them there. Second Chronicles 30:5-11 and 34:6-9 suggest that a few Jews escaped deportation, but even these must have mingled with the imported groups and so lost any Jewish identity.

Question 10. Numerous factors influenced the people of Israel and the newly formed Samaritans toward idolatry. Find a dozen or so in verses 14-17 and 24-33.

Questions 11-12. Save at least ten minutes for these final application questions. Encourage several group members to respond as honestly as is practical. After others have spoken, be ready to share some of your own thinking on the subject.

In all of history, we never again see this nation, Israel. In fact, it is often called "the ten lost tribes."

Study 9. Hezekiah: King in Crisis. Isaiah 36—37.
Purpose: To turn to God in crisis—rather than away from him.

Question 2. Find Lachish on the map. (It is *south* of Jerusalem, indicating that Assyria was already in charge of much Judean territory.) Notice the three men representing King Hezekiah and the field commander representing the king of Assyria. "The Upper Pool, on the road to the Washerman's Field" (v. 2) is the same one where Isaiah had met King Ahaz (Is 7:3). It was the source of the city's water supply. Hezekiah, however, sometime during his reign built an alternate source for water. (See 2 Chron 32:2-4, 30 and 2 Kings 20:20.)

Question 3. See also 2 Kings 18:13-16. "Excavations at Lachish, which Sennacherib stormed, reveal, along with evidences of destruction, a huge pit into which the remains of some 1,500 bodies had been dumped and covered with pig bones and other debris—presumably the garbage of the Assyrian army" (Bright, p. 286).

Question 4. Find twisted truth throughout the passage. Your group should touch on the ways he tried to undermine their faith in political allies (Egypt), their faith in King Hezekiah, their faith in God.

Question 5. If you have extra time, also ask, "If you had been King Hezekiah, newly informed about this meeting, what would you have done?"

Question 6. Taunts about God appear in verses 16, 18 and 20.

Question 8. Use information throughout verses 1-20. Notice the constant reference to God's power as compared to military power. Even the military movements of Egypt brought renewed Assyrian ire on Hezekiah. Your group should notice the spiritual threats behind this new warning from Sennacherib.

You may wonder whether Sennacherib waged one campaign against Jerusalem or two. There is no easy answer. For a thorough treatment of the problem read John Bright's *A History of Israel,* pages 298-309.

Question 9. Allow enough time for your group to examine the high quality of worship in Hezekiah's prayer, though Hezekiah did not deny the critical circumstances he faced. Even so, his purpose for requesting help was an evangelistic vindication of God's character: "So that all kingdoms on earth may know that you alone, O LORD, are God" (v. 20).

Question 10. Don't spend undue time on this question. Just invite several people to select a brief phrase or concept that they might call their own.

Question 11. Your group should find many ways in which this story attacks the Assyrian accusations. There is particular irony in comparing Isaiah 36:10, "The LORD himself told me to march against this country and destroy it," with 37:26-27. The Assyrian's words were more true than he realized, yet God would turn that same sovereign power back on the Assyrians (see v. 29).

Your group may also notice the irony of the Assyrian question "On whom are you depending?" (36:5), when viewed in light of the whole thrust of this song, "Whom have you mocked?"

If you have time for additional questions, try, "Compare 37:26-27 with the Assyrian taunt of 36:10. In what ways was the field commander correct? How was his perspective limited?"

Question 14. Allow a minute or two for group members to record their thoughts. Then suggest that people cup what they have written into their hands and offer the crisis to God in a brief vocal or silent prayer. Close with your own brief spoken prayer on behalf of the group.

Study 10. Manasseh: One Giant Step Backward. 2 Kings 20:1—21:18.
Purpose: To trust God even when we can see no positive results of our work for him.

Question 2. Your group should find many details in these verses that show what kind of relationship they had.

There is no hint in this passage that it was inappropriate for Hezekiah to request a sign. In Isaiah 7:10-12, Ahaz was invited by God to request a sign. (He refused but got one anyway.)

Did the earth stop in its orbit and turn backward? "Not likely," say most commentators. *New Bible Commentary* is typical of much scholarly opinion: "Whether the sun was actually moved backward, or some refraction of its rays caused its shadow to move backward, is a discussion based on attempts to find more than the biblical text actually says" (William Sanford, "1 and 2 Kings," in *The New Bible Commentary*, 3rd. ed., rev., ed. D. Guthrie et al. [Downers Grove, Ill.: InterVarsity Press, 1970], p. 364).

Question 3. Use your map to find geographic relationships between Assyria, Babylon and Judah. This is the first biblical reference to Babylon except in 2 Kings 17 where its people are captives of Assyria.

Hezekiah may have had any number of reasons, some admirable, some not: (1) he may have wanted a political alliance with natural enemies of Assyria, (2) he may have been exhibiting pride in his possessions (2 Chron 32:25-26 suggests this), or (3) he may have wanted to show trust and honor to messengers from royalty.

Question 5. Why did Hezekiah not appeal once again to God for the deliverance of his people? God had saved the people from Assyria but now declares that Babylon will conquer them instead. Perhaps Hezekiah lacked the energy to continue fighting. Perhaps he already saw the evil that his son Manasseh would bring to the land. Or, perhaps, since these words came from God and not some foreign pagan, he simply trusted them as good and right—and died a peaceful death.

Question 7. Notice the quote of the promise given to the people during Solomon's dedication of the temple, and the conditions (for the people) attached to it (vv. 7-8).

Verse 9 says the *people* did not listen. Verse 15 sums up God's view of the actions of his people. Notice that this is in no way limited to the era of Manasseh.

Question 8. Notice the symbol of the plumb line (also mentioned in Amos 7:7 as a prophecy against the northern kingdom), the wiped dish, the term *remnant*, the ominous references to Samaria (whose people already were deported to Assyria) and the house of Ahab.

Question 10. Note on verse 16: "Josephus . . . says that Manasseh slew some every day. According to tradition he slew Isaiah the prophet, sawing him asunder" (*New Bible Commentary*, p. 365).

Question 11. This question is not as straightforward as it seems. True, Manasseh was born in that fifteen years, but prior to that, Hezekiah had fathered no sons—and so his death would have ended a 250-year line of Davidic kings.

In addition, by comparing 18:2, 13 and 20:6, we find that Hezekiah's illness must have occurred just *prior* to the siege of Sennacherib. If he had died during that illness, he would have left the throne vacant at a critical time. Sharp-eyed readers may notice that the text does not say that Hezekiah asked for an extension to his life. God simply responded to his tearful prayer by giving it.

Study 11. Josiah: Following God's Law. 2 Kings 22:1—23:30.
Purpose: To practice respect for God's law.
Question 5. It is interesting to note that Hezekiah also celebrated Passover as part of his reform. (See 2 Chron 30.) But Hezekiah did not have the benefit of specific instructions for Passover from the Book of the Law. And his animal sacrifices were only one-tenth of those recorded for Josiah. Second Chronicles 35:7 states that the sacrificial animals came from Josiah's own possessions.

If you want more information on "the man who came from Judah" in 23:17, read 1 Kings 13.
Question 8. If the question of New Testament law versus Old Testament law comes into the discussion in this or a later question, you could comment that Old Testament law is often divided into three categories: ceremonial law, civil law and moral law. New Testament Christians need only be bound by the moral law of the Old Testament. But distinguishing what is moral law from the other two categories is no small task.
Question 11. If you want the discussion to take a more personal direction, ask: "Think back on your own responses to God's law. Try to think of a specific standard of behavior that you became aware of rather suddenly. What were your first feelings about that law?" For an alternate question or a follow-up question, ask, "Why is the term *law,* even if it belongs to God, hard for us to live with?"
Question 12. If time permits ask also, "What does the fact that God sets standards of behavior for his people reveal about the character of God?"

Study 12. Zedekiah: End of the Line. 2 Kings 24:1—25:21.
Purpose: To accept God's kind sovereignty over the events of history.
Question 3. Help your group tell in sequence the outline of events recorded here.
Question 6. Your group will probably remember with pathos Hezekiah's actions in 2 Kings 20:12-18. The godly kings Hezekiah and Josiah were each followed by sons who took the nation away from God. Why? *New Bible*

Commentary says: "We must ask ourselves, Why? Hezekiah forgot to ask the Lord before he opened his treasury to the Babylonians, and Josiah forgot to ask whether he should go to Megiddo—is there any connection?" (p. 366).

Question 8. Encourage a brief sentence of response from each person present.

Question 9. Lead a time of prayer for the national needs and leaders mentioned in response to question 8.

Questions 10-12. Use these questions from Jeremiah 29 to end your study on a note of hope.

After the End of the Line

If your group would like to telescope nearly 600 years ahead in time, they will find new people in the same places. Read Matthew 1:6b—2:12. There you will find a list of the kings, with a few more names added at the end. And you will find God's people once again living near Jerusalem. Important visitors from the East (Babylon?) come to see a new Hebrew king. His name is Immanuel: God with us.

Carolyn Nystrom is an editor of adult education at Victor Books. She has written over 55 children's books and Bible study guides, including six Christian Character Bible Studies and the LifeGuides® 1 & 2 Peter and Jude and New Testament Characters. She and her husband, Roger, live in St. Charles, Illinois, with an assortment of cats and kids and quilts.